Producer & International Distributor
eBookPro Publishing
www.ebook-pro.com

THE EXPRESS PASSOVER HAGGADAH: The Simple Family-Friendly Haggadah for
a Short But Meaningful Passover Seder
MILAH TOVAH PRESS

Cover & Illustrations: Maria Sokhatski
Editor: Dani Silas

Contact: agency@ebook-pro.com
ISBN **9798871402184**

HOW TO USE THIS HAGGADAH

The purpose of The Express Passover Haggadah is to allow you and your family and friends to enjoy a concise, meaningful Passover Seder without skipping the most important parts.

This modern Haggadah is a shortened version of the long traditional one, with all the beloved, familiar texts and blessings that will make your Seder night a reverent and enjoyable experience.

All Hebrew blessings and texts are translated and transliterated for easy reading and the Haggadah is laid out in a way that will make it easy for everyone to follow along.

Icons alongside the text will help orient you and clarify what needs to be done next:

   Appears next to instructions

   Lets you know when a blessing should be recited

   Appears in relation to the four cups of wine

You can find all of your favorite Passover songs (Chad Gadya, Who Knows One?, Go Down Moses) all together in the *Songs* chapter, so you can skip back and forth and incorporate them in your Seder as you go along.

If there will be children at your Passover Seder night, make sure to take a look at our children's version of the Haggadah – The Passover Haggadah for Kids. This special Haggadah includes fun activities and work pages to keep children engaged and occupied throughout the night.

THE ORDER OF THE SEDER

THE SEDER PLATE

ZERO'A

typically a lamb shank bone, often substituted for cooked chicken

MAROR

a bitter vegetable, usually horseradish or lettuce

BEITZAH

a hard-boiled egg

CHAROSET

a sweet paste made with apples and nuts

KARPAS

a green leafy vegetable, usually parsley or celery

HAZERET

more of the same or a different bitter vegetable

MATZAH

beside the seder plate, we place three whole matzahs, which will play an important part in the Seder

KADESH קַדֵשׁ

Blessing on the Wine

KADESH קַדֵּשׁ

 During the Seder, we will drink four cups of wine, to symbolize the four ways that God rescued us from slavery:

He **extracted** us from Egypt, **saved** us from the Egyptians, **redeemed** us from our suffering and **united** us as a nation.

 We begin the Seder by drinking the first cup of wine, and we make the traditional blessing on the wine:

בָּרוּךְ אַתָּה יְיָ אֱלֹהֵינוּ מֶלֶךְ הָעוֹלָם בּוֹרֵא פְּרִי הַגָּפֶן.

Baruch atah Adonai Eloheinu melech ha-olam, borei peri ha-gafen.

Blessed are You, Lord our G-d, King of the universe, creator of the fruit of the vine.

We also thank God for allowing us to celebrate this joyous occasion with friends and family!

בָּרוּךְ אַתָּה יְיָ אֱלֹהֵינוּ מֶלֶךְ הָעוֹלָם, שֶׁהֶחֱיָנוּ וְקִיְּמָנוּ וְהִגִּיעָנוּ לַזְּמַן הַזֶּה.

Baruch atah Adonai Eloheinu melech ha-olam, sh'hecheyanu v'kiyemanu v'higiyanu l'zman hazeh.

Blessed are You, Lord our G-d, King of the universe, who has given us life, sustained us, and allowed us to reach this time.

URCHATZ וּרְחַץ

Washing Hands

URCHATZ וּרְחַץ

 Wash your hands using a washing cup, pouring water three times onto each hand. Do not recite a blessing.

This is a traditional way of washing our hands that we do before eating, to remind us of the rules of purity that were observed during Temple times.

KARPAS כַּרְפַּס

The Leafy Vegetable

KARPAS כַּרְפַּס

☞ Take some karpas (parsley, celery, or another leafy green vegetable) and dip it into salt water.

📜 Recite the blessing:

בָּרוּךְ אַתָּה יְיָ אֱלֹהֵינוּ מֶלֶךְ
הָעוֹלָם, בּוֹרֵא פְּרִי הָאֲדָמָה.

Baruch atah Adonai Eloheinu Melech ha-olam, borei peri ha-adamah.

Blessed are You, Lord our G-d, King of the universe, creator of the fruit of the earth.

☞ After reciting the blessing, eat the karpas.

Why do we eat a leafy vegetable right at the beginning of the Seder? And why must we dip it into salt water?

The answer to that question is simple – the night of Passover is all about asking questions. We want adults and children alike to be engaged and involved, to show interest in the story of the Exodus, and to be invested in their legacy as Jews.

So we start off with something a little strange, that we don't do every day – simply to kickstart the Seder with a curiosity, something to make us wonder about.

YACHATZ יַחַץ

Breaking the Middle Matzah

YACHATZ יַחַץ

Remember those three matzahs that we put aside at the beginning of the evening, right next to the Seder plate?

 Now, take the middle one and break it into two.

Don't try to break it perfectly in half, as we want to have one piece bigger than the other. This imperfection is symbolic, and comes to represent the People of Israel, before and after the Exodus.

The smaller, more humble piece reminds us of our humble beginnings as slaves in Egypt. We had little to nothing, and lived in poverty.

The larger piece, which will go on to play an important part in the Seder, represents our forefathers who were redeemed from Egypt and saved from slavery. It symbolizes abundance and gratitude for all the wonderful things that we have.

 Take the larger piece and set it aside. This will be our Afi-koman.

If you have kids participating in your Seder, it is customary at this point for the leader of the seder to wrap up the Afikoman and hide it somewhere for younger participants to find later.

This fun custom not only keeps kids involved in the Seder, but also helps make sure they don't get bored!

 Now, return the smaller piece of the middle matzah to its place between the first and third matzahs.

MAGID מַגִּיד

Telling the Story
of Exodus

MAGID מַגִּיד

"Magid", or in Hebrew, "he who tells", is our opportunity as Jewish people to keep alive the memory of how we became a nation. So, it is traditional to tell the story of our Exodus from Egypt and the chain of events that brought us to where we are today – a strong, united people with a rich history and tradition.

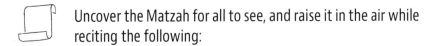 Uncover the Matzah for all to see, and raise it in the air while reciting the following:

הָא לַחְמָא עַנְיָא דִי אֲכָלוּ
אַבְהָתָנָא בְּאַרְעָא דְמִצְרָיִם.

Ha lachma anya, di achalu avha-
tana b'ar'a d'mitsrayim.

This is the bread of poverty that our ancestors ate in the land of Egypt.

All who are hungry may come and eat, all who are in need may come and celebrate with us.

Today we are here, here's to next year in the land of Israel. Today we are slaves, here's to next year as a free people.

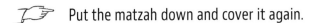 Put the matzah down and cover it again.

Then pour everyone a second cup of wine.

MAH NISHTANAH – WHAT IS DIFFERENT?

It is traditional for the youngest participant of each Seder to ask the four questions, with the rest of the participants replying. We want children to be curious about their roots, to question what they see and hear.

So, we allow them the opportunity to ask about all the strange things we are doing tonight – eating dry matzah instead of bread, eating leafy vegetables instead of a real salad, dipping things in salt water, and reclining to the left as we eat and drink.

מַה נִּשְׁתַּנָה הַלַּיְלָה הַזֶּה מִכָּל הַלֵּילוֹת ?

Mah nishtanah halaylah hazeh mikol haleylot?

שֶׁבְּכָל הַלֵּילוֹת אָנוּ אוֹכְלִין חָמֵץ וּמַצָּה, הַלַּיְלָה הַזֶּה - כֻּלּוֹ מַצָּה.

She-b'kol haleylot anu ochlin chametz u'matzah, halaylah hazeh – kulo matzah.

שֶׁבְּכָל הַלֵּילוֹת אָנוּ אוֹכְלִין שְׁאָר יְרָקוֹת, - הַלַּיְלָה הַזֶּה מָרוֹר.

She-b'kol haleylot anu ochlin she'ar yerakot, halaylah hazeh – maror.

שֶׁבְּכָל הַלֵּילוֹת אֵין אָנוּ מַטְבִּילִין אֲפִילוּ פַּעַם אֶחָת, - הַלַּיְלָה הַזֶּה שְׁתֵּי פְעָמִים.

She-b'kol haleylot eyn anu matbilin afilu pa'am achat, halaylah hazeh – shtey pe'amim.

שֶׁבְּכָל הַלֵּילוֹת אָנוּ אוֹכְלִין בֵּין יוֹשְׁבִין וּבֵין מְסֻבִּין, - הַלַּיְלָה הַזֶּה כֻּלָּנוּ מְסֻבִּין.

She-b'kol haleylot anu ochlin beyn yoshvin u'beyn mesubin, halaylah hazeh – kulanu mesubin.

What makes this night different from any other night?
On every other night we eat chametz and matzah. On this night – only matzah.
On every other night we eat all kinds of vegetables. On this night – only maror.
On every other night we do not dip our vegetables even once. On this

night – we dip twice.

On every other night we eat reclining and sitting straight. On this night – we all recline.

עֲבָדִים הָיִינוּ לְפַרְעֹה בְּמִצְרָיִם   Avadim hayinu l'paroh b'mits-rayim

We were slaves of Pharoah in Egypt, until the Lord our G-d took us out from there with a strong hand and an outstretched arm. Had G-d, blessed be His name, not liberated our ancestors from Egypt, we and our sons and daughters and their sons and daughters would still be enslaved to Pharoah in Egypt today.

We remember the miracles that G-d bestowed upon us in liberating us from Egypt all those years ago.

THE FOUR CHILDREN

כְּנֶגֶד אַרְבָּעָה בָנִים דִּבְּרָה תוֹרָה.
אֶחָד חָכָם, וְאֶחָד רָשָׁע, וְאֶחָד
תָּם, וְאֶחָד שֶׁאֵינוֹ יוֹדֵעַ לִשְׁאוֹל.

Ke-neged arba'ah banim dibrah torah. Echad chacham, v'echad rasha, v'echad tam, v'echad she'eyno yode'a lishol.

The Torah tells us of four children.

One who is **wise**, one who is **wicked**, one who is simple, and one who is too young or timid to ask.

19

What does the wise child say?

The wise child is involved. They want to know more about their legacy, they are eager and willing to hear the story. They say to their parents: "What are these rules and rituals that the Lord our G-d has commanded you?", wanting to be a part of the celebrations.

So, you will teach this child the tale of Passover and how to celebrate the Seder and all its rules.

What does the wicked child say?

The wicked child does not see him or herself as one of the group. They look on with disdain at the strange and unexplained rituals of Passover, and ask: "What are these rules you follow?"

The wicked child does not care.

So, you shall tell him: we tell this story to remember what G-d did for us when He liberated us from Egypt. We hope that telling this child about our fascinating history will encourage curiosity and empathy.

What does the simple child say?

The simple child does not understand much. He or she sees the Seder plate, the funny matzahs, and the unfamiliar rituals of Passover and just asks, "What's all this?"

So you shall tell this child: G-d liberated us with a mighty hand from Egypt and from slavery.

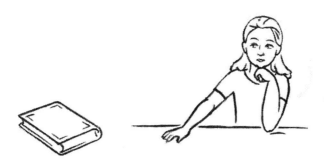

And what about the child who is too young or timid to ask?

It is your responsibility to interest this young child in the story, to tell them the story of the Haggadah and capture their interest and imagination.

THE TEN PLAGUES

אֵלּוּ עֶשֶׂר מַכּוֹת שֶׁהֵבִיא הַקָּדוֹשׁ
בָּרוּךְ הוּא עַל הַמִּצְרִים בְּמִצְרַיִם,
וְאֵלּוּ הֵן:

Eylu eser ha-makot she-hevi ha-
Kadosh Baruch Hu al ha-mitsrim
b'mitsrayim, v'eylu hen:

These are the ten plagues that G-d, Blessed be His Name, brought
down upon the Egyptians in Egypt:

 As you recite the ten plagues, pour a drop of wine from your
cup onto a plate for each.

דָּם Dam **Blood**

צְפַרְדֵּעַ Tsfardeya **Frogs**

כִּנִּים Kinim **Lice**

עָרוֹב Arov **Wild Beasts**

דֶּבֶר Dever **Plague**

שְׁחִין Shechin **Boils**

בָּרָד Barad **Hail**

אַרְבֶּה Arbeh **Locusts**

חֹשֶׁךְ Choshech **Darkness**

מַכַּת בְּכוֹרוֹת Makat Bechorot
Slaying of the Firstborn

רַבִּי יְהוּדָה הָיָה נוֹתֵן בָּהֶם
סִמָנִים:

Rabi Yehudah hayah noten ba-hem simanim:

Rabbi Yehuda would assign them mnemonics:

דְּצַ"ךְ	Detsach (blood, frogs, lice)
עַדַ"שׁ	Adash (wild beasts, plague, boils)
בְּאַחַ"ב	B'achav (hail, locusts, darkness, slaying of the firstborn)

Pour another drop of wine for each of the three mnemonics.

Remove the cup of wine and the plate with the wine you spilled and refill your second cup of wine.

DAYEINU

כַּמָּה מַעֲלוֹת טוֹבוֹת לַמָּקוֹם עָלֵינוּ!

Kama ma'alot tovot la-makom aleynu!

אִלּוּ הוֹצִיאָנוּ מִמִּצְרַיִם וְלֹא עָשָׂה בָהֶם שְׁפָטִים, דַּיֵּנוּ.

Ilu hotsi'anu m'mitsrayim v'lo asah vahem shefatim, dayeinu.

אִלּוּ עָשָׂה בָהֶם שְׁפָטִים, וְלֹא עָשָׂה בֵאלֹהֵיהֶם, דַּיֵּנוּ.

Ilu asah behm shefatim v'lo asah b'eloheyhem, dayeinu.

אִלּוּ עָשָׂה בֵאלֹהֵיהֶם, וְלֹא הָרַג אֶת בְּכוֹרֵיהֶם, דַּיֵּנוּ.

Ilu asah b'eloheyhem v'lo harag et bechoreyhem, dayeinu.

אִלּוּ הָרַג אֶת בְּכוֹרֵיהֶם וְלֹא נָתַן לָנוּ אֶת מָמוֹנָם, דַּיֵּנוּ.

Ilu harag et bechoreyhem v'lo natan lanu et mamonam, dayeinu.

אִלּוּ נָתַן לָנוּ אֶת מָמוֹנָם וְלֹא קָרַע לָנוּ אֶת הַיָּם, דַּיֵּנוּ.

Ilu natan lanu et mamonam v'lo kara lanu et hayam, dayeinu.

אִלּוּ קָרַע לָנוּ אֶת הַיָּם וְלֹא הֶעֱבִירָנוּ בְתוֹכוֹ בֶּחָרָבָה, דַּיֵּנוּ.

Ilu kara lanu et hayam v'lo he'eyviranu betocho b'charavah, dayeinu.

אִלּוּ הֶעֱבִירָנוּ בְתוֹכוֹ בֶּחָרָבָה וְלֹא שִׁקַּע צָרֵנוּ בְּתוֹכוֹ, דַּיֵּנוּ.

Ilu he'eyviranu betocho b'chara-vah v'lo shika tsareynu betocho, dayeinu.

אִלּוּ שִׁקַּע צָרֵנוּ בְּתוֹכוֹ וְלֹא סִפֵּק צָרְכֵּנוּ בַּמִּדְבָּר אַרְבָּעִים שָׁנָה, דַּיֵּנוּ.

Ilu shika tsareynu betocho v'lo sipek tsarcheynu ba-midbar ar-ba'im shanah, dayeinu.

אִלּוּ סִפֵּק צָרְכֵּנוּ בַּמִּדְבָּר אַרְבָּעִים שָׁנָה וְלֹא הֶאֱכִילָנוּ אֶת הַמָּן, דַּיֵּנוּ.

Ilu sipek tsarcheynu ba-midbar arba'im shanah v'lo he'eychila-nu et ha-man, dayeinu.

אִלּוּ הֶאֱכִילָנוּ אֶת הַמָּן וְלֹא נָתַן לָנוּ אֶת הַשַּׁבָּת, דַּיֵּינוּ.	Ilu he'eychilanu et ha-man v'lo natan lanu et ha-shabbat, dayeinu.
אִלּוּ קֵרְבָנוּ לִפְנֵי הַר סִינַי, וְלֹא נָתַן לָנוּ אֶת הַתּוֹרָה, דַּיֵּינוּ.	Ilu natan lanu et ha-shabbat v'lo kervanu lifney har sinai, dayeinu.
אִלּוּ נָתַן לָנוּ אֶת הַשַּׁבָּת, וְלֹא קֵרְבָנוּ לִפְנֵי הַר סִינַי, דַּיֵּינוּ.	Ilu kervanu lifney har sinai v'lo natan lanu et ha-torah, dayeinu.
אִלּוּ נָתַן לָנוּ אֶת הַתּוֹרָה וְלֹא הִכְנִיסָנוּ לְאֶרֶץ יִשְׂרָאֵל, דַּיֵּינוּ.	Ilu natan lanu et ha-torah v'lo hichnisanu l'eretz yisrael, dayeinu.
אִלּוּ הִכְנִיסָנוּ לְאֶרֶץ יִשְׂרָאֵל וְלֹא בָנָה לָנוּ אֶת בֵּית הַבְּחִירָה, דַּיֵּינוּ.	Ilu hichnisanu l'eretz Yisrael v'lo vana lanu et beyt ha-behira, dayeinu.

How many good favors G-d has bestowed upon us!

Had He liberated us from Egypt and not carried out justice against the Egyptians, we would have been grateful enough.

Had He carried out justice against the Egyptians and not against their gods, we would have been grateful enough.

Had He carried out justice against their gods and not slain their first-borns, we would have been grateful enough.

Had He slain their firstborns and not given us their treasures, we would have been grateful enough.

Had He given us their treasures and not split the sea for us, we would have been grateful enough.

Had He split the sea for us and not let us through it on dry land, we would have been grateful enough.

Had He led us through the sea on dry land and not drowned our enemies in it, we would have been grateful enough.

Had He drowned our enemies in the sea and not provided for us in the desert for forty years, we would have been grateful enough.

Had He provided for us in the desert for forty years and not given us the manna, we would have been grateful enough.

Had He given us the manna and not given us the Sabbath, we would have been grateful enough.

Had He given us the Sabbath and not brought us to Mount Sinai, we would have been grateful enough.

Had He brought us to Mount Sinai and not given us the Torah, we would have been grateful enough.

Had He given us the Torah and not brought us into Israel, we would have been grateful enough.

Had He brought us into Israel and not built the Temple of worship, we would have been grateful enough.

Rabbi Gamliel would say, all who have not recited these three things on Passover have not done their duty. And these things are:

☞ All say together:

פֶּסַח, מַצָּה, וּמָרוֹר. Pesach, matzah, u'maror.

Pesach, Matzah, and Bitter Herbs.

Pesach, the sacrificial offering that our ancestors would eat while the Temple was standing. What is the meaning of it?

In the time of the Temple, Jews would congregate in Jerusalem three times a year – on Passover, on Pentecost, and on Sukkot. On Passover, they would bring with them an offering of a lamb in memory of the doors the Israelites painted in blood to signify their homes, so that G-d would only smite the firstborns of the Egyptians, sparing the Jews.

☞ Raise the matzah and say:

Matzah, this unleavened bread that we eat, what is the meaning of it?

The matzah that we eat throughout the week of Passover symbolizes the unleavened bread that our ancestors made and did not have time to rise before they had to rush out of Egypt.

Raise the maror and say:

Maror, these bitter herbs that we eat, what is the meaning of it?

In memory of the bitterness that the Egyptians inflicted on the lives of our ancestors. The Torah says: "and they made their lives bitter with hard labor, with mortar and bricks, work in the fields and every form of slavery that they forced upon them."

In every generation, we all must see ourselves as though we ourselves were liberated from Egypt.

"And on that day, you shall tell your child all that G-d did for you when He set you free from Egypt. "

 Drink the second cup of wine, reclining to the left.

RACHTZAH רַחְצָה

Washing Hands
(this time, with a blessing)

RACHTZAH רַחְצָה

Wash your hands again, pouring water from a cup onto each hand three times.

This time, recite the blessing, because you are about to eat matzah:

בָּרוּךְ אַתָּה יְיָ אֱלֹהֵינוּ מֶלֶךְ הָעוֹלָם, אֲשֶׁר קִדְּשָׁנוּ בְּמִצְוֹתָיו וְצִוָּנוּ עַל נְטִילַת יָדָיִם.

Baruch atah Adonai Eloheinu melech ha-olam, asher kideshanu b'mitzvotav v'tzivanu al netilat yadayim.

Blessed are You, Lord our G-d, King of the universe, who has sanctified us with His commandments and commanded us to wash our hands.

When we wash our hands a second time, we are preparing to eat Matzah for the first time this Passover. On a regular Shabbat and other Jewish occasions, we wash our hands before we eat challah, the traditional Jewish braided bread.

On Passover, because we do not eat any bread that has risen, we substitute challah for matzah.

מוֹצִיא מַצָּה
MOTZI-MATZAH
Blessing on the Matzah

MOTZI-MATZAH מוֹצִיא מַצָּה

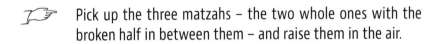

Pick up the three matzahs – the two whole ones with the broken half in between them – and raise them in the air.

First, recite the blessing on the bread:

בָּרוּךְ אַתָּה יְיָ אֱלֹהֵינוּ מֶלֶךְ הָעוֹלָם הַמּוֹצִיא לֶחֶם מִן הָאָרֶץ.

Baruch atah Adonai Eloheinu melech ha-olam, ha-motzi lechem min ha-aretz.

Blessed are You, Lord our G-d, King of the universe, who produces bread from the earth.

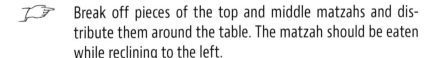

Now, remove the bottom matzah from the pile and return it to its place. Holding only the top and middle matzahs, recite the following blessing – the blessing on eating matzah:

בָּרוּךְ אַתָּה יְיָ אֱלֹהֵינוּ מֶלֶךְ הָעוֹלָם, אֲשֶׁר קִדְּשָׁנוּ בְּמִצְוֹתָיו וְצִוָּנוּ עַל אֲכִילַת מַצָּה.

Baruch atah Adonai Eloheinu melech ha-olam, asher kideshanu b'mitzvotav v'tzivanu al achilat matzah.

Blessed are You, Lord our G-d, King of the universe, who has sanctified us with His commandments and commanded us to eat matzah.

Break off pieces of the top and middle matzahs and distribute them around the table. The matzah should be eaten while reclining to the left.

MAROR מָרוֹר

Bitter Herb

MAROR מָרוֹר

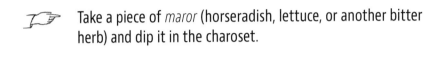 Take a piece of *maror* (horseradish, lettuce, or another bitter herb) and dip it in the charoset.

Recite the blessing before eating:

בָּרוּךְ אַתָּה יְיָ אֱלֹהֵינוּ מֶלֶךְ
הָעוֹלָם, אֲשֶׁר קִדְּשָׁנוּ בְּמִצְוֹתָיו
וְצִוָּנוּ עַל אֲכִילַת מָרוֹר.

Baruch atah Adonai Eloheinu melech ha-olam, asher kide-shanu b'mitzvotav v'tzivanu al achilat maror.

Blessed are You, Lord our G-d, King of the universe, who has sancti-fied us with His commandments and commanded us to eat a bitter herb.

KORECH כּוֹרֵךְ

Maror Wrapped
in Matzah

KORECH כּוֹרֵךְ

☞ Take two pieces of matzah, put some maror between them, and dip everything in the charoset. You may also spread the charoset on the matzah, add the maror and eat it like a sandwich.

Recite before eating:

In memory of the custom of Hillel in the days of the Temple. So Hillel would do while there was a Temple: he would wrap the matzah with the maror and the Passover sacrifice and eat them together, to observe what is commanded: You shall eat it (the Passover sacrifice) on matzah and maror.

Recline to the left and eat the maror sandwich.

שֻׁלְחָן עוֹרֵךְ
SHULCHAN-ORECH
The Festive Meal

SHULCHAN-ORECH שֻׁלְחָן עוֹרֵךְ

☞ Now is the time to sit back, relax, and enjoy a delicious festive meal.

☞ At this point, it is customary to eat the hard-boiled egg from the Seder plate, dipped in salt water.

The egg dipped in salt water signifies the tears of the ancient Israelites who cried over the destruction of the Temple.

Even when we are happy and rejoicing, we remember the tragedy that befell our people centuries ago.

Judaism is all about remembering. We remember both the good and the bad, the tragic and the uplifting, the recent and the ancient. Even our most joyous ceremonies are often punctuated by solemn moments of remembrance, such as the breaking of the cup under the chuppah during a Jewish wedding, to signify the fall of the Temple.

TZAFUN צָפוּן

The Afikoman

TZAFUN צָפוּן

☞ Now that you've finished the meal, it's time to reveal the Afikoman.

☞ If you hid it earlier in the evening, now is the time for who-ever found it during the Seder to return it, but not before asking for something in exchange!

The Afikoman is the last thing we eat during the Seder night. Break off pieces of the Afikoman matzah and distribute them around the table. Eat the matzah while reclining to your left.

BARECH בָּרֵךְ

Blessing After the Meal

BARECH בָּרֵךְ

  Pour the third cup of wine.

  Recite, for the third time, the blessing on the wine:

בָּרוּךְ אַתָּה יְיָ אֱלֹהֵינוּ מֶלֶךְ
הָעוֹלָם בּוֹרֵא פְּרִי הַגָּפֶן.

Baruch atah Adonai Eloheinu melech ha-olam, borei peri ha-gafen.

Blessed are You, Lord our G-d, King of the universe, creator of the fruit of the vine.

  Drink the third cup of wine, while reclining to the left.

  Pour everyone a fourth cup of wine.

When you pour the fourth cup of wine, it is customary to pour an extra cup of wine for Elijah the Prophet, who is said to visit on Seder night. Open the front door to invite him in.

אֵלִיָהוּ הַנָּבִיא, אֵלִיָהוּ הַתִּשְׁבִּי,
אֵלִיָהוּ הַגִּלְעָדִי, בִּמְהֵרָה יָבֹא
אֵלֵינוּ עִם מָשִׁיחַ בֶּן דָּוִד.

Eliyahu ha-navi, Eliyahu ha-tish-bi, Eliyahu ha-giladi. Bimheirah yavo eleynu, im Mashiach ben David.

May Elijah the prophet, Elijah the Tishbite, Elijah of Gilead, quickly in our day come to us heralding redemption with the Messiah, son of David.

HALLEL הַלֵּל

Praise to G-d

HALLEL הַלֵּל

 Make a final blessing on the fourth cup of wine:

בָּרוּךְ אַתָּה יְיָ אֱלֹהֵינוּ מֶלֶךְ
הָעוֹלָם בּוֹרֵא פְּרִי הַגָּפֶן.

Baruch atah Adonai Eloheinu melech ha-olam, borei peri ha-gafen.

Blessed are You, Lord our G-d, King of the universe, creator of the fruit of the vine.

 Drink the fourth and final cup of wine while reclining to the left.

NIRTZAH נִרְצָה

Conclusion of the Seder

NIRTZAH נִרְצָה

At the conclusion of the Seder, we celebrate having been able to come together for the festivities and look forward to a prosperous and happy year ahead.

👉 Everyone sings together:

לְשָׁנָה הַבָּאָה בִּירוּשָׁלָיִם.   L'shana haba'ah b'Yerushalayim

Next year in Jerusalem!

We don't pray necessarily to celebrate next year in the physical city of Jerusalem, rather we pray for the unification of the Jewish people and the rebuilding of the Temple.

We can think of the Temple not as a material thing or place, but as a oneness, a freedom to be who we are, to believe in what we wish to believe, and to celebrate and rejoice in the uniqueness of our being Jews.

SONGS

Chad Gadya – One Little Goat

חַד גַּדְיָא, חַד גַּדְיָא, דְּזַבִּין אַבָּא
בִּתְרֵי זוּזֵי, חַד גַּדְיָא,חַד גַּדְיָא.

Chad gadya, chad gadya, d'zabin aba b'trei zuzei, chad gadya, chad gadya.

וְאָתָא שׁוּנְרָא וְאָכְלָה לְגַדְיָא,
דְּזַבִּין אַבָּא בִּתְרֵי זוּזֵי, חַד גַּדְיָא,
חַד גַּדְיָא.

V'ata shunra v'achla l'gadya, d'zabin aba b'trei zuzei, chad gadya, chad gadya.

וְאָתָא כַלְבָּא וְנָשַׁךְ לְשׁוּנְרָא,
דְּאָכְלָה לְגַדְיָא, דְּזַבִּין אַבָּא בִּתְרֵי
זוּזֵי, חַד גַּדְיָא,חַד גַּדְיָא.

V'ata chalba v'nashach l'shunra, d'achla l'gadya, d'zabin aba b'trei zuzei, chad gadya, chad gadya.

וְאָתָא חוּטְרָא וְהִכָּה לְכַלְבָּא,
דְּנָשַׁךְ לְשׁוּנְרָא, דְּאָכְלָה לְגַדְיָא,
דְּזַבִּין אַבָּא בִּתְרֵי זוּזֵי, חַד
גַּדְיָא,חַד גַּדְיָא.

V'ata chutra v'hica l'calba, d'nashach l'shunra, d'achla l'gadya, d'zabin aba b'trei zuzei, chad gadya, chad gadya.

וְאָתָא נוּרָא וְשָׂרַף לְחוּטְרָא,
דְּהִכָּה לְכַלְבָּא, דְּנָשַׁךְ לְשׁוּנְרָא,
דְּאָכְלָה לְגַדְיָא, דְּזַבִּין אַבָּא בִּתְרֵי
זוּזֵי, חַד גַּדְיָא, חַד גַּדְיָא

V'ata nura v'saraf l'chutra, d'hica l'calba, d'nashach l'shunra, d'achla l'gadya, d'zabin aba b'trei zuzei, chad gadya, chad gadya.

וְאָתָא מַיָּא וְכָבָה לְנוּרָא, דְּשָׂרַף
לְחוּטְרָא, דְּהִכָּה לְכַלְבָּא, דְּנָשַׁךְ
לְשׁוּנְרָא, דְּאָכְלָה לְגַדְיָא, דְּזַבִּין
אַבָּא בִּתְרֵי זוּזֵי, חַד גַּדְיָא,חַד
גַּדְיָא.

V'ata maya v'chaba l'nura, d'saraf l'chutra, d'hica l'calba, d'nashach l'shunra, d'achla l'gadya, d'zabin aba b'trei zuzei, chad gadya, chad gadya.

וְאָתָא תוֹרָא וְשָׁתָה לְמַיָא, דְּכָבָה לְנוּרָא, דְּשָׂרַף לְחוּטְרָא, דְּהִכָּה לְכַלְבָּא, דְּנָשַׁךְ לְשׁוּנְרָא, דְּאָכְלָה לְגַדְיָא, דְּזַבִּין אַבָּא בִּתְרֵי זוּזֵי, חַד גַּדְיָא, חַד גַּדְיָא.

V'ata tora v'shata l'maya, d'chaba l'nura, d'saraf l'chutra, d'hica l'calba, d'nashach l'shunra, d'achla l'gadya, d'zabin aba b'trei zuzei, chad gadya, chad gadya.

וְאָתָא הַשּׁוֹחֵט וְשָׁחַט לְתוֹרָא, דְּשָׁתָה לְמַיָא, דְּכָבָה לְנוּרָא, דְּשָׂרַף לְחוּטְרָא, דְּהִכָּה לְכַלְבָּא, דְּנָשַׁךְ לְשׁוּנְרָא, דְּאָכְלָה לְגַדְיָא, דְּזַבִּין אַבָּא בִּתְרֵי זוּזֵי, חַד גַּדְיָא, חַד גַּדְיָא.

V'ata hashochet v'shachat l'tora, d'shata l'maya, d'chaba l'nura, d'saraf l'chutra, d'hica l'calba, d'nashach l'shunra, d'achla l'gadya, d'zabin aba b'trei zuzei, chad gadya, chad gadya.

וְאָתָא מַלְאַךְ הַמָּוֶת וְשָׁחַט לְשׁוֹחֵט, דְּשָׁחַט לְתוֹרָא, דְּשָׁתָה לְמַיָא, דְּכָבָה לְנוּרָא, דְּשָׂרַף לְחוּטְרָא, דְּהִכָּה לְכַלְבָּא, דְּנָשַׁךְ לְשׁוּנְרָא, דְּאָכְלָה לְגַדְיָא, דְּזַבִּין אַבָּא בִּתְרֵי זוּזֵי, חַד גַּדְיָא, חַד גַּדְיָא.

V'ata malach hamavet v'shachat l'shochet, d'shachat l'tora, d'shata l'maya, d'chaba l'nura, d'saraf l'chutra, d'hica l'calba, d'nashach l'shunra, d'achla l'gadya, d'zabin aba b'trei zuzei, chad gadya, chad gadya.

וְאָתָא הַקָּדוֹשׁ בָּרוּךְ הוּא וְשָׁחַט לְמַלְאַךְ הַמָּוֶת, דְּשָׁחַט לְשׁוֹחֵט, דְּשָׁחַט לְתוֹרָא, דְּשָׁתָה לְמַיָא, דְּכָבָה לְנוּרָא, דְּשָׂרַף לְחוּטְרָא, דְּהִכָּה לְכַלְבָּא, דְּנָשַׁךְ לְשׁוּנְרָא, דְּאָכְלָה לְגַדְיָא דְּזַבִּין אַבָּא בִּתְרֵי זוּזֵי, חַד גַּדְיָא, חַד גַּדְיָא.

V'ata ha-Kadosh Baruch Hu, v'ishachat l'malach hamavet, d'shachat l'shochet, d'shachat l'tora, d'shata l'maya, d'chaba l'nura, d'saraf l'chutra, d'hica l'calba, d'nashach l'shunra, d'achla l'gadya, d'zabin aba b'trei zuzei, chad gadya, chad gadya.

One little goat, one little goat that father bought for two zuzim. One little goat, one little goat.

Along came a cat and ate the goat that father bought for two zuzim. One little goat, one little goat.

Along came a dog and bit the cat that ate the goat that father bought for two zuzim. One little goat, one little goat.

Along came a stick and hit the dog that bit the cat that ate the goat that father bought for two zuzim. One little goat, one little goat.

Along came a fire and burned the stick that hit the dog that bit the cat that ate the goat that father bought for two zuzim. One little goat, one little goat.

Along came some water and put out the fire that burned the stick that hit the dog that bit the cat that ate the goat that father bought for two zuzim. One little goat, one little goat.

Along came an ox and drank the water that put out the fire that burned the stick that hit the dog that bit the cat that ate the goat that father bought for two zuzim. One little goat, one little goat.

Along came a butcher and slaughtered the ox that drank the water that put out the fire that burned the stick that hit the dog that bit the cat that ate the goat that father bought for two zuzim. One little goat, one little goat.

Along came the angel of death and slaughtered the butcher who slaughtered the ox that drank the water that put out the fire that burned the stick that hit the dog that bit the cat that ate the goat that father bought for two zuzim. One little goat, one little goat.

Then along came the Holy One, Blessed be He, and slaughtered the angel of death who slaughtered the butcher who slaughtered the ox that drank the water that put out the fire that burned the stick that hit the dog that bit the cat that ate the goat that father bought for two zuzim. One little goat, one little goat.

Echad Mi Yodeya – Who Knows One?

אֶחָד מִי יוֹדֵעַ? אֶחָד אֲנִי יוֹדֵעַ. אֶחָד אֱלֹהֵינוּ שֶׁבַּשָּׁמַיִם וּבָאָרֶץ.

Echad mi yodea? Echad ani yodea. Echad Eloheinu she-bashamayim u'va'aretz.

שְׁנַיִם מִי יוֹדֵעַ? שְׁנַיִם אֲנִי יוֹדֵעַ. שְׁנֵי לוּחוֹת הַבְּרִית, אֶחָד אֱלֹהֵינוּ שֶׁבַּשָּׁמַיִם וּבָאָרֶץ.

Shnayim mi yodea? Shnayim ani yodea. Shnei luchot ha-brit, echad Eloheinu she-bashamayim u'va'aretz.

שְׁלֹשָׁה מִי יוֹדֵעַ? שְׁלֹשָׁה אֲנִי יוֹדֵעַ. שְׁלֹשָׁה אָבוֹת, שְׁנֵי לוּחוֹת הַבְּרִית, אֶחָד אֱלֹהֵינוּ שֶׁבַּשָּׁמַיִם וּבָאָרֶץ.

Shloshah mi yodea? Shloshah ani yodea. Shloshah avot, shnei luchot ha-brit, echad Eloheinu she-bashamayim u'va'aretz.

אַרְבַּע מִי יוֹדֵעַ? אַרְבַּע אֲנִי יוֹדֵעַ. אַרְבַּע אִמָּהוֹת, שְׁלֹשָׁה אָבוֹת, שְׁנֵי לוּחוֹת הַבְּרִית, אֶחָד אֱלֹהֵינוּ שֶׁבַּשָּׁמַיִם וּבָאָרֶץ.

Arbah mi yodea? Arbah ani yodea. Arbah imahot, shloshah avot, shnei luchot ha-brit, echad Eloheinu she-bashamayim u'va'aretz.

חֲמִשָּׁה מִי יוֹדֵעַ? חֲמִשָּׁה אֲנִי יוֹדֵעַ. חֲמִשָּׁה חֻמְשֵׁי תוֹרָה, אַרְבַּע אִמָּהוֹת, שְׁלֹשָׁה אָבוֹת, שְׁנֵי לוּחוֹת הַבְּרִית, אֶחָד אֱלֹהֵינוּ שֶׁבַּשָּׁמַיִם וּבָאָרֶץ.

Chamishah mi yodea? Chamishah ani yodea. Chamishah chumshei Torah, arbah imahot, shloshah avot, shnei luchot ha-brit, echad Eloheinu she-bashamayim u'va'aretz.

שִׁשָּׁה מִי יוֹדֵעַ? שִׁשָּׁה אֲנִי יוֹדֵעַ. שִׁשָּׁה סִדְרֵי מִשְׁנָה, חֲמִשָּׁה חֻמְשֵׁי תוֹרָה, אַרְבַּע אִמָּהוֹת, שְׁלֹשָׁה אָבוֹת שְׁנֵי לוּחוֹת הַבְּרִית, אֶחָד אֱלֹהֵינוּ שֶׁבַּשָּׁמַיִם וּבָאָרֶץ.

Shishah mi yodea? Shishah ani yodea. Shishah sidrei mishnah, chamishah chumshei Torah, arbah imahot, shloshah avot, shnei luchot ha-brit, echad Eloheinu she-bashamayim u'va'aretz.

שִׁבְעָה מִי יוֹדֵעַ? שִׁבְעָה אֲנִי יוֹדֵעַ. שִׁבְעָה יְמֵי שַׁבַּתָּא, שִׁשָּׁה סִדְרֵי מִשְׁנָה, חֲמִשָּׁה חֻמְשֵׁי תוֹרָה, אַרְבַּע אִמָּהוֹת, שְׁלֹשָׁה אָבוֹת, שְׁנֵי לֻחוֹת הַבְּרִית, אֶחָד אֱלֹהֵינוּ שֶׁבַּשָּׁמַיִם וּבָאָרֶץ.

Shivah mi yodea? Shivah ani yodea. Shivah y'mei shabtah, shishah sidrei mishnah, chamishah chumshei Torah, arbah imahot, shloshah avot, shnei luchot ha-brit, echad Eloheinu she-bashamayim u'va'aretz.

שְׁמוֹנָה מִי יוֹדֵעַ? שְׁמוֹנָה אֲנִי יוֹדֵעַ. שְׁמוֹנָה יְמֵי מִילָה, שִׁבְעָה יְמֵי שַׁבַּתָּא, שִׁשָּׁה סִדְרֵי מִשְׁנָה, חֲמִשָּׁה חֻמְשֵׁי תוֹרָה, אַרְבַּע אִמָּהוֹת, שְׁלֹשָׁה אָבוֹת, שְׁנֵי לֻחוֹת הַבְּרִית, אֶחָד אֱלֹהֵינוּ שֶׁבַּשָּׁמַיִם וּבָאָרֶץ.

Shmonah mi yodea? Shmonah ani yodea. Shmonah y'mei milah, shivah y'mei shabtah, shishah sidrei mishnah, chamishah chumshei Torah, arbah imahot, shloshah avot, shnei luchot ha-brit, echad Eloheinu she-bashamayim u'va'aretz.

תִּשְׁעָה מִי יוֹדֵעַ? תִּשְׁעָה אֲנִי יוֹדֵעַ. תִּשְׁעָה יַרְחֵי לֵדָה, שְׁמוֹנָה יְמֵי מִילָה, שִׁבְעָה יְמֵי שַׁבַּתָּא, שִׁשָּׁה סִדְרֵי מִשְׁנָה, חֲמִשָּׁה חֻמְשֵׁי תוֹרָה, אַרְבַּע אִמָּהוֹת, שְׁלֹשָׁה אָבוֹת, שְׁנֵי לֻחוֹת הַבְּרִית, אֶחָד אֱלֹהֵינוּ שֶׁבַּשָּׁמַיִם וּבָאָרֶץ.

Tishah mi yodea? Tishah ani yodea. Tishah yarchei leidah, shmonah y'mei milah, shivah y'mei shabtah, shishah sidrei mishnah, chamishah chumshei Torah, arbah imahot, shloshah avot, shnei luchot ha-brit, echad Eloheinu she-bashamayim u'va'aretz.

עֲשָׂרָה מִי יוֹדֵעַ? עֲשָׂרָה אֲנִי יוֹדֵעַ. עֲשָׂרָה דִבְּרַיָּא, תִּשְׁעָה יַרְחֵי לֵדָה, שְׁמוֹנָה יְמֵי מִילָה, שִׁבְעָה יְמֵי שַׁבַּתָּא, שִׁשָּׁה סִדְרֵי מִשְׁנָה, חֲמִשָּׁה חֻמְשֵׁי תוֹרָה, אַרְבַּע אִמָּהוֹת, שְׁלֹשָׁה אָבוֹת, שְׁנֵי לֻחוֹת הַבְּרִית, אֶחָד אֱלֹהֵינוּ שֶׁבַּשָּׁמַיִם וּבָאָרֶץ.

Asarah mi yodea? Asarah ani yodea. Asarah dibrayah, tishah yarchei leidah, shmonah y'mei milah, shivah y'mei shabtah, shishah sidrei mishnah, chamishah chumshei Torah, arbah imahot, shloshah avot, shnei luchot ha-brit, echad Eloheinu she-bashamayim u'va'aretz.

אַחַד עָשָׂר מִי יוֹדֵעַ? אַחַד עָשָׂר
אֲנִי יוֹדֵעַ. אַחַד עָשָׂר כּוֹכְבַיָּא,
עֲשָׂרָה דִּבְּרַיָּא, תִּשְׁעָה יַרְחֵי
לֵדָה, שְׁמוֹנָה יְמֵי מִילָה, שִׁבְעָה
יְמֵי שַׁבַּתָּא, שִׁשָּׁה סִדְרֵי מִשְׁנָה,
חֲמִשָּׁה חֻמְשֵׁי תוֹרָה, אַרְבַּע
אִמָּהוֹת, שְׁלֹשָׁה אָבוֹת, שְׁנֵי
לוּחוֹת הַבְּרִית, אֶחָד אֱלֹהֵינוּ
שֶׁבַּשָּׁמַיִם וּבָאָרֶץ.

Achad-asar mi yodea? Achad-asar ani yodea. Achad-asar kochvayah, asarah dibrayah, tishah yarchei leidah, shmonah y'mei milah, shivah y'mei shabtah, shishah sidrei mishnah, chamishah chumshei Torah, arbah imahot, shloshah avot, shnei luchot ha-brit, echad Eloheinu she-bashamayim u'va'aretz.

שְׁנֵים עָשָׂר מִי יוֹדֵעַ? שְׁנֵים
עָשָׂר אֲנִי יוֹדֵעַ. שְׁנֵים עָשָׂר
שִׁבְטַיָּא, אַחַד עָשָׂר כּוֹכְבַיָּא,
עֲשָׂרָה דִּבְּרַיָּא, תִּשְׁעָה יַרְחֵי
לֵדָה, שְׁמוֹנָה יְמֵי מִילָה, שִׁבְעָה
יְמֵי שַׁבַּתָּא, שִׁשָּׁה סִדְרֵי מִשְׁנָה,
חֲמִשָּׁה חֻמְשֵׁי תוֹרָה, אַרְבַּע
אִמָּהוֹת, שְׁלֹשָׁה אָבוֹת, שְׁנֵי
לוּחוֹת הַבְּרִית, אֶחָד אֱלֹהֵינוּ
שֶׁבַּשָּׁמַיִם וּבָאָרֶץ.

Shneim-asar mi yodea? Shneim-asar ani yodea. Shneim-asar shivtayah, achad-asar kochvayah, asarah dibrayah, tishah yarchei leidah, shmonah y'mei milah, shivah y'mei shabtah, shishah sidrei mishnah, chamishah chumshei Torah, arbah imahot, shloshah avot, shnei luchot ha-brit, echad Eloheinu she-bashamayim u'va'aretz.

שְׁלֹשָׁה עָשָׂר מִי יוֹדֵעַ? שְׁלֹשָׁה
עָשָׂר אֲנִי יוֹדֵעַ. שְׁלֹשָׁה עָשָׂר
מִדַּיָּא, שְׁנֵים עָשָׂר שִׁבְטַיָּא, אַחַד
עָשָׂר כּוֹכְבַיָּא, עֲשָׂרָה דִּבְּרַיָּא,
תִּשְׁעָה יַרְחֵי לֵדָה, שְׁמוֹנָה יְמֵי
מִילָה, שִׁבְעָה יְמֵי שַׁבַּתָּא, שִׁשָּׁה
סִדְרֵי מִשְׁנָה, חֲמִשָּׁה חֻמְשֵׁי
תוֹרָה, אַרְבַּע אִמָּהוֹת, שְׁלֹשָׁה
אָבוֹת, שְׁנֵי לוּחוֹת הַבְּרִית, אֶחָד
אֱלֹהֵינוּ שֶׁבַּשָּׁמַיִם וּבָאָרֶץ.

Shloshah-asar mi yodea? Shloshah-asar ani yodea. Shloshah-asar midayah, shneim-asar shivtayah, achad-asar kochvayah, asarah dibrayah, tishah yarchei leidah, shmonah y'mei milah, shivah y'mei shabtah, shishah sidrei mishnah, chamishah chumshei Torah, arbah imahot, shloshah avot, shnei luchot ha-brit, echad Eloheinu she-bashamayim u'va'aretz.

Who knows one? I know one. One is our G-d in Heaven and Earth.

Who knows two? I know two. Two are the tablets of the covenant. One is our G-d in Heaven and Earth.

Who knows three? I know three. Three are the patriarchs. Two are the tablets of the covenant. One is our G-d in Heaven and Earth.

Who knows four? I know four. Four are the matriarchs. Three are the patriarchs. Two are the tablets of the covenant. One is our G-d in Heaven and Earth.

Who knows five? I know five. Five are the books of the Torah. Four are the matriarchs. Three are the patriarchs. Two are the tablets of the covenant. One is our G-d in Heaven and Earth.

Who knows six? I know six. Six are the orders of the Mishnah. Five are the books of the Torah. Four are the matriarchs. Three are the patriarchs. Two are the tablets of the covenant. One is our G-d in Heaven and Earth.

Who knows seven? I know seven. Seven are the days of the week. Six are the orders of the Mishnah. Five are the books of the Torah. Four are the matriarchs. Three are the patriarchs. Two are the tablets of the covenant. One is our G-d in Heaven and Earth

Who knows eight? I know eight. Eight are the days for circumcision. Seven are the days of the week. Six are the orders of the Mishnah. Five are the books of the Torah. Four are the matriarchs. Three are the patriarchs. Two are the tablets of the covenant. One is our G-d in Heaven and Earth.

Who knows nine? I know nine. Nine are the months of childbirth. Eight are the days for circumcision. Seven are the days of the week.

Six are the orders of the Mishnah. Five are the books of the Torah. Four are the matriarchs. Three are the patriarchs. Two are the tablets of the covenant. One is our G-d in Heaven and Earth.

Who knows ten? I know ten. Ten are the Words from Sinai. Nine are the months of childbirth. Eight are the days for circumcision. Seven are the days of the week. Six are the orders of the Mishnah. Five are the books of the Torah. Four are the matriarchs. Three are the patriarchs. Two are the tablets of the covenant. One is our G-d in Heaven and Earth.

Who knows eleven? I know eleven. Eleven are the stars. Ten are the Words from Sinai. Nine are the months of childbirth. Eight are the days for circumcision. Seven are the days of the week. Six are the orders of the Mishnah. Five are the books of the Torah. Four are the matriarchs. Three are the patriarchs. Two are the tablets of the covenant. One is our G-d in Heaven and Earth.

Who knows twelve? I know twelve. Twelve are the tribes. Eleven are the stars. Ten are the Words from Sinai. Nine are the months of childbirth. Eight are the days for circumcision. Seven are the days of the week. Six are the orders of the Mishnah. Five are the books of the Torah. Four are the matriarchs. Three are the patriarchs. Two are the tablets of the covenant. One is our G-d in Heaven and Earth.

Who knows thirteen? I know thirteen. Thirteen are the attributes of G-d. Twelve are the tribes. Eleven are the stars. Ten are the Words from Sinai. Nine are the months of childbirth. Eight are the days for circumcision. Seven are the days of the week. Six are the orders of the Mishnah. Five are the books of the Torah. Four are the matriarchs. Three are the patriarchs. Two are the tablets of the covenant. One is our G-d in Heaven and Earth.

Let My People Go

"When Israel was in Egypt land, let my people go.
Oppressed so hard they could not stand, let my people go."
Go down, Moses, way down in Egypt land.
Tell old Pharaoh, let my people go!

"Thus saith the Lord" bold Moses said, "Let my people go,
If not I'll smite your firstborn dead, let my people go."
Go down, Moses, way down in Egypt land.
Tell old Pharaoh, let my people go!

"No more shall they in bondage toil, let my people go.
Let them come out with Egypt's spoils, let my people go."
Go down, Moses, way down in Egypt land.
Tell old Pharaoh, let my people go!

"When people stop this slavery, let my people go.
Soon may all the earth be free, let my people go."
Go down, Moses, way down in Egypt land.
Tell old Pharaoh, let my people go!

Made in the USA
Columbia, SC
14 April 2025

56636255R00035